A New True Book

YOUR HEART AND BLOOD

By Leslie Jean LeMaster

This "true book" was prepared under the direction of
William H. Wehrmacher, M. D. FACC, FACP
Clinical Professor of Medicine and
Adjunct Professor of Physiology
Loyola University Stritch School of Medicine
with the help of his granddaughter Cheryl Sabey

CHILDRENS PRESS ™

CHICAGO

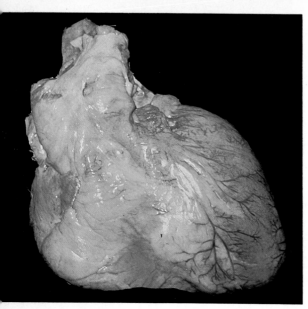

Human heart

PHOTO CREDITS

©L.V. Bergman & Associates, Inc.—Cover 2, 6, 15 (2 photos), 23 (2 photos), 36, 37

Wide World—39

Museum of Science and Industry, Chicago—4 (2 photos), 19

Allan Roberts—34

©Denoyer-Geppert—17 (bottom), 27

Hillstrom Stock Photos—©Brooks & Van Kirk, 41 (bottom left)

©Tony Freeman—8, 20 (top), 43, 44

©Joseph DiChello, Jr.—41 (top left)

©EKM-Nepenthe—photos by Tom Ballard, 10, 20 (bottom right), 29 (2 photos), 32, 42 (2 photos)

Nawrocki Stock Photos—©Phylane Norman, 20 (bottom left), 45; ©Jim Whitmer, 41 (right); ©Larry Brooks, 31

Len Meents—12, 13, 17

COVER—Human heart, showing blood vessels

Library of Congress Cataloging in Publication Data

LeMaster, Leslie Jean.
  Your heart and blood.

  (A New true book)
  Summary: Discusses the composition of the blood and its importance to body function and describes the structure of the heart and its role in pumping the blood through the body.
  Includes index.
  1. Heart—Juvenile literature. 2. Blood—Juvenile literature. [1. Heart. 2. Blood] I. Title.
QP111.6.L46 1984   612'.1   84-7604
ISBN 0-516-01933-3   AACR2

TABLE OF CONTENTS

At the Museum of Science and Industry in Chicago, Illinois, people can walk through this giant model of the human heart.

WHAT IS BLOOD?

Have you ever wondered what your heart looks like or how it works? Do you know why you need blood? Do you know how blood travels through your body and what special work it does?

Blood is made up of a liquid called plasma, many red cells, fewer white cells, and platelets. The red cells

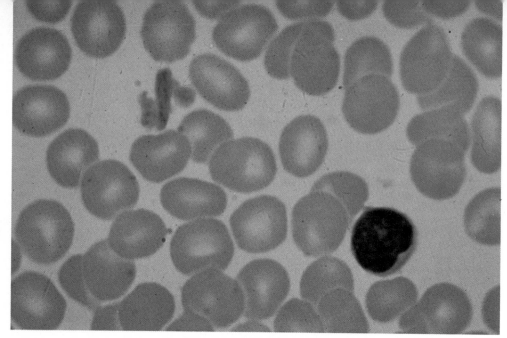

Blood is made up of red blood cells, white blood cells, and platelets.

give blood its red color. The white cells kill harmful germs in the blood. And the platelet cells make blood thicken or clot when you get a cut. This stops the cut from bleeding too much.

WHY DOES A CUT BLEED?

When skin is cut open it
bleeds. This is because
part of a blood vessel
(a tube that carries blood)
under the skin is also
cut open.

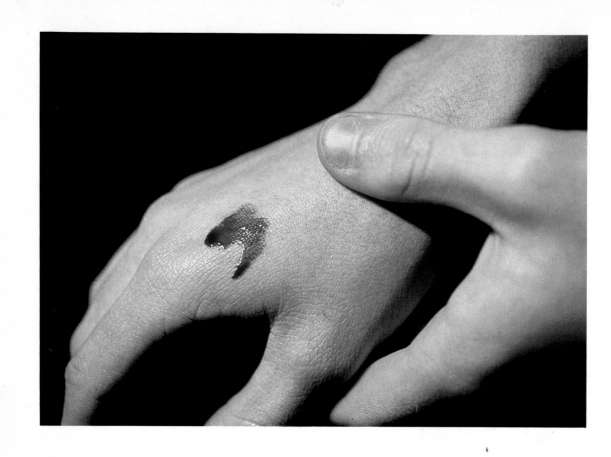

Bleeding usually stops
quickly when only small
blood vessels are cut.
But if large blood vessels
are cut, bleeding can be
heavy and hard to stop.

WHAT IS A BRUISE?

When you bump your knee, you've probably noticed that later a black-and-blue mark often appears. This dark-colored mark or bruise is a sign of bleeding under the skin. A small part of a blood vessel may break open. But if the skin doesn't

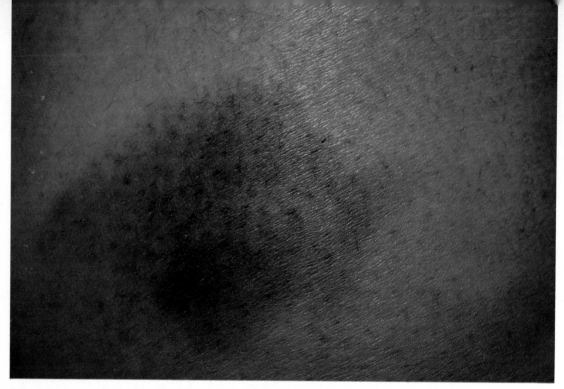

A bruise is a sign of bleeding under the skin.

break open, blood can't
get out. So this blood
stays under the skin. Its
red color changes to black
and blue and later to
green and yellow before
it goes away.

WHAT DOES BLOOD DO?

In addition to killing germs and stopping cuts from bleeding too much, blood also works to carry food and oxygen to all the cells in your body. This is how the cells stay healthy. Food and oxygen get into the cells by passing through the walls of the blood vessels.

Blood also cleans the cells by carrying waste

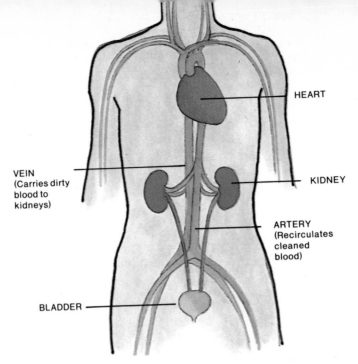

HEART

VEIN
(Carries dirty
blood to
kidneys)

KIDNEY

ARTERY
(Recirculates
cleaned
blood)

BLADDER

material out of them. The
wastes pass from the cells
through the walls of the
blood vessels into the
blood. The blood carries
these wastes to the
kidneys. Then the wastes
leave the body in the form
of urine.

HOW MUCH BLOOD IS IN YOUR BODY?

A child who weighs about fifty pounds has about one and a half quarts of blood in its body. But when that child becomes an adult, its body will hold about five to six quarts of blood.

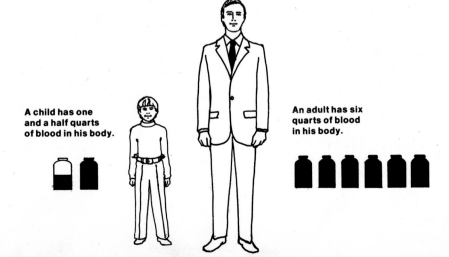

A child has one and a half quarts of blood in his body.

An adult has six quarts of blood in his body.

WHAT ARE BLOOD VESSELS?

Your blood travels through your whole body in less than one minute. This happens more than a thousand times every day. Blood travels through tubes called blood vessels. The three most important kinds of blood vessels are arteries, veins, and capillaries.

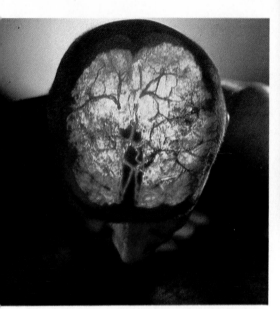
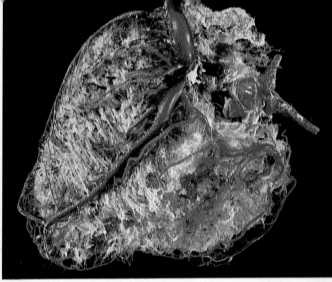

Blood vessels in the brain (left) and
blood vessels in the heart (above)

Arteries carry blood
away from the heart. Veins
carry blood to the heart.
Capillaries are tiny blood
vessels that connect the
arteries with the veins so
your blood travels in a
complete circle (the
circulation).

WHAT DOES YOUR HEART LOOK LIKE?

Your heart is not really the shape of a valentine heart. It is about the shape and size of your fist. It is located in the middle and slightly toward the left side of the chest.

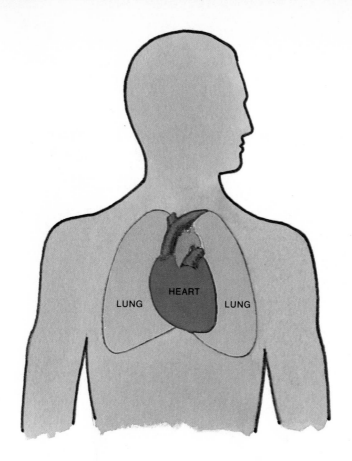

LUNG   HEART   LUNG

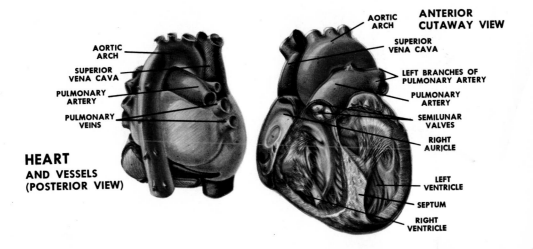

AORTIC
ARCH

SUPERIOR
VENA CAVA

PULMONARY
ARTERY

PULMONARY
VEINS

HEART
AND VESSELS
(POSTERIOR VIEW)

AORTIC
ARCH

**ANTERIOR
CUTAWAY VIEW**

SUPERIOR
VENA CAVA

LEFT BRANCHES OF
PULMONARY ARTERY

PULMONARY
ARTERY

SEMILUNAR
VALVES

RIGHT
AURICLE

LEFT
VENTRICLE

SEPTUM

RIGHT
VENTRICLE

WHAT DOES YOUR HEART DO?

Your heart is the pump that moves the blood through your body. It is made up of muscle tissue that first tightens and then relaxes as it pumps blood. This activity of the heart is called a heartbeat. If the heart did not beat, blood would not move, or circulate, through the body.

The sound of a heartbeat comes from the

Students walk through human heart model.

opening and closing of valves as the heart beats. These valves work like one-way doors. They let blood in or out of the heart. The valves close after letting blood pass through them so that blood cannot back up and travel in the wrong direction.

Your heart beats faster
when you exercise.
It has a slower beat
when you are sleeping
or resting.

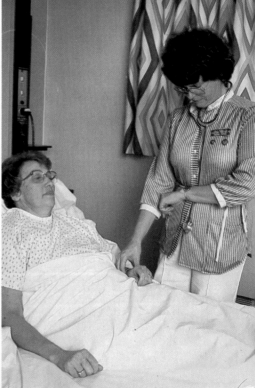

HOW FAST DOES YOUR HEART BEAT?

Your heart beats about eighty to ninety times a minute when you are normally active. It beats faster when you exercise. It beats slower when you sleep. When you become an adult, your heart will beat about seventy to eighty times a minute when you are normally active.

21

HOW DOES THE HEART PUMP YOUR BLOOD?

Your heart beats all your life without stopping. But between each heartbeat, your heart rests for a moment. While it is resting, it is filling with blood.

The heart is divided into four sections called chambers. There are two upper chambers, or

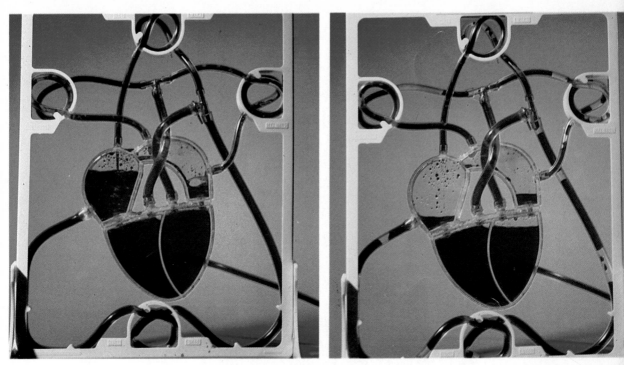

The auricles, the upper chambers of the heart (left), fill with blood when the heart rests. When the heart beats (right), the blood is pumped into the ventricles, the lower chambers, and out to all parts of the body.

auricles. One auricle is on the right side. The other is on the left side.

There are also two lower chambers, or ventricles.

One ventricle is on the right side, the other on the left side.

The upper chambers beat first. This forces blood into the lower chambers. When the lower chambers fill with blood, they beat to pump blood out into all parts of the body. Then the heart rests for a moment while the upper chambers again fill with blood.

WHERE DOES BLOOD GO AS IT TRAVELS THROUGH YOUR BODY?

Blood is carried through your body in a certain way.

The right ventricle beats. This forces blood into a large artery that carries the blood to the lungs.

The red cells in the blood take oxygen from

the air breathed into the lungs. From the lungs, blood is carried back to the heart through veins. The blood then enters the left auricle. It passes through a valve into the left ventricle.

The left ventricle beats. This forces blood into another large artery. This artery divides into smaller and smaller arteries. The smallest arteries are called capillary arteries. From the

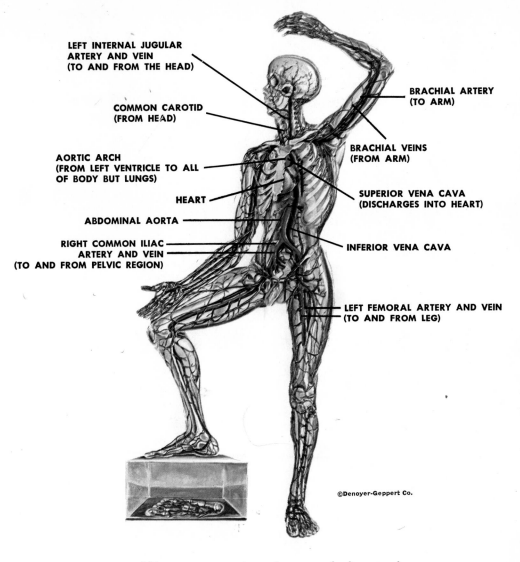

LEFT INTERNAL JUGULAR
ARTERY AND VEIN
(TO AND FROM THE HEAD)

COMMON CAROTID
(FROM HEAD)

AORTIC ARCH
(FROM LEFT VENTRICLE TO ALL
OF BODY BUT LUNGS)

HEART

ABDOMINAL AORTA

RIGHT COMMON ILIAC
ARTERY AND VEIN
(TO AND FROM PELVIC REGION)

BRACHIAL ARTERY
(TO ARM)

BRACHIAL VEINS
(FROM ARM)

SUPERIOR VENA CAVA
(DISCHARGES INTO HEART)

INFERIOR VENA CAVA

LEFT FEMORAL ARTERY AND VEIN
(TO AND FROM LEG)

©Denoyer-Geppert Co.

capillary arteries, blood
carries food and oxygen to
body cells. The blood also

removes carbon dioxide and other wastes from the cells.

The tiny capillary arteries connect with tiny capillary veins. These veins connect with larger and larger veins as they lead nearer to the heart. Blood is carried to a large vein that leads to the right auricle of the heart.

From the right auricle, blood passes through a valve into the right ventricle.

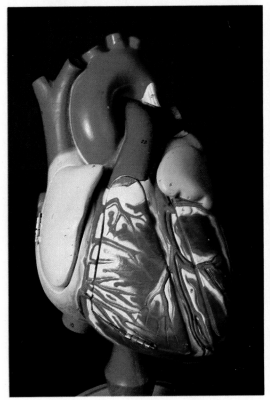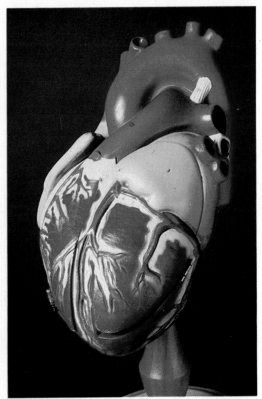

Model of human heart

Your blood has now
made one complete trip
through your body. This is
repeated more than a
thousand times every day
of your life.

AMAZING FACTS: WOULD YOU BELIEVE THAT...?

The heart beats more than 100,000 times every day and about 42 million times every year.

The heart rests for a moment between individual heartbeats. The total amount of time the heart rests in one day adds up to more than five hours.

When you grow up, your heart will pump about

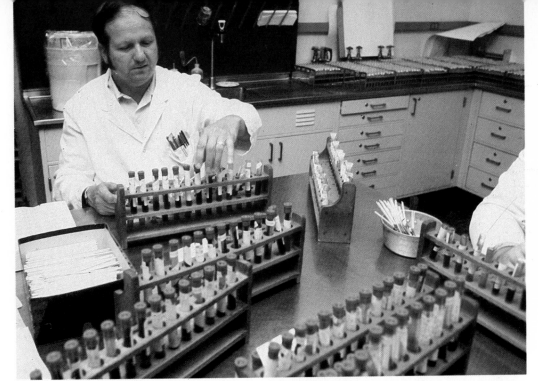

Testing blood samples in laboratory

10,000 quarts or 2,500
gallons of blood each day.
 Hospitals have blood
banks where blood from
healthy people is kept.
Sometimes sick or injured
people lose too much of

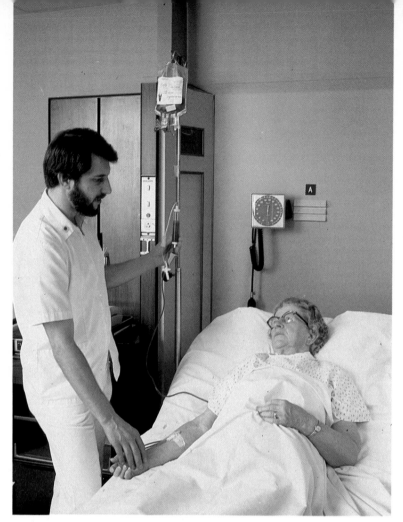

Patient receives blood.

their own blood. Then a
blood bank gives them the
blood they need to get
better.

People have different
blood types. If you were
given blood that was not
the same type as your own,
your blood cells would die.

There. are four main
blood types—A, B, AB, and
O. Each type of blood is
either positive or negative.
If your blood is positive, you
have what is called the Rh
factor. (*Rh* stands for *rhesus*.
Rhesus monkeys were used
in blood-testing research.

Rhesus monkey

The Rh factor was first
discovered in these
monkeys.)

If all your capillaries
were arranged in a straight
line, they would measure a
distance of over fifteen
thousand miles.

Red blood cells are so small that if one hundred of them were arranged side by side, they would fit on a dot this size (.).

When you grow up, your blood will contain about 35 billion (35,000,000,000) red cells!

About 5 million old red blood cells die and 5 million new red blood cells are made each second.

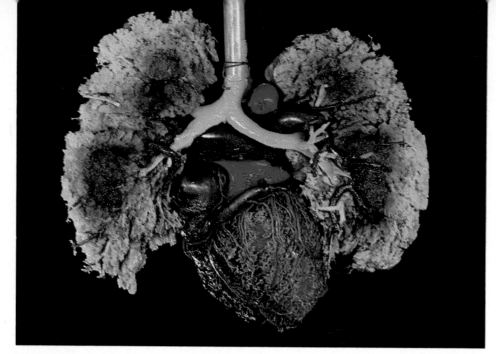

Heart and lungs

Each red cell lives only about 120 days.

You breathe over ten thousand quarts of air in and out of your lungs every day. That much air would blow up more than one thousand balloons.

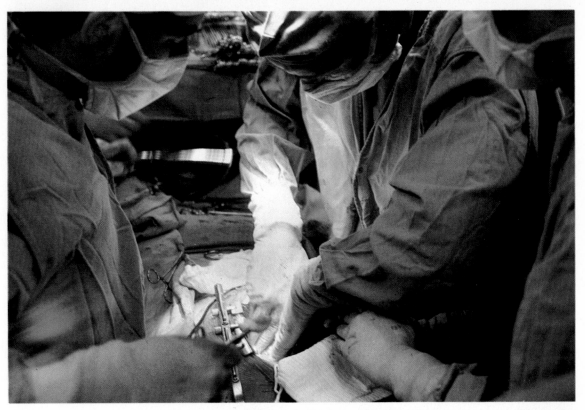

Surgeons can operate to repair some damaged hearts.

Sometimes a person's heart becomes too diseased or sick to work properly. Scientists have invented a new kind of heart made of plastic.

In 1983 a man named Barney Clark was dying from heart disease. Doctors removed his heart and put in a plastic one.

The new heart was connected to a machine by tubes. The machine sent compressed air to the plastic heart to make it beat. Barney Clark lived with his new heart for two months. Then the heart stopped working.

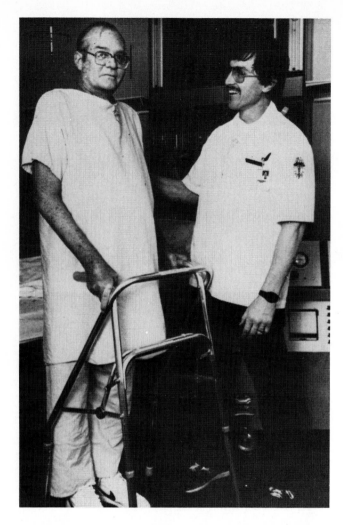

Barney Clark (left)
was the first
human to receive
a plastic heart.

Barney Clark made
medical history because he
was the first person to live
with a plastic heart.

KEEP YOUR HEART HEALTHY !

Your heart is the most important organ in your body. Body cells need food and oxygen to stay alive. Your heart pumps the blood that carries food and oxygen to the cells.

Many diseases can stop a heart from working properly.

Eating the right foods can keep your heart healthy

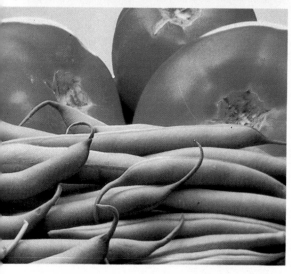

You can do things to help your heart stay healthy. Eat foods low in fats, sugar, and salt. Get

Exercise and rest are also needed to keep your heart healthy.

plenty of exercise. Get
enough sleep. Stay away
from cigarette smoke and
harmful drugs.

If your heart is healthy, it
will do its best work!

Remember. . . .

YOUR HEART PUMPS
 BLOOD TO EVERY
 CELL,
SO THAT YOUR BODY
 WILL FUNCTION WELL.

WORDS YOU SHOULD KNOW

arteries(ARE • tuh • reez) — tubes that carry blood away from the heart to other parts of the body

auricles(AW • ric • kuls) — the upper right and left chambers of the heart

blood vessels(BLUD VES • ilz) — tubes that carry blood to all parts of your body

bruise(BROOZ) — bleeding from a broken blood vessel under the skin

capillaries(CAP • ih • lair • eez) — tiny tubes that connect the arteries and veins

carbon dioxide(CAR • bun dy • OX • ide) — a gas formed in body tissues and released by the lungs as waste

cell(SELL) — the basic structural unit of life

circulation(sir • cue • LAY • shun) — movement of blood through the body in a certain pattern

clot(KLOT) — blood that thickens in the area of an open cut so that the blood will stop flowing out of the cut

heartbeat(HART • beet) — the constant movement of the heart squeezing and relaxing as it pumps blood

organ(OR • gan) — a group of the same kind of tissues that work together to do a certain job

oxygen(OX • ih • gen) — a gas in the air we breathe into our lungs which is carried by blood to body cells

plasma(PLAZ • mah) — the light yellow liquid part of blood

platelets(PLAYT • letz) — round-shaped cells in blood that work to stop bleeding from open cuts

tissue(TISH • u) — a group of the same kind of cells that work together to do a certain job

urine(YOOR • in) — fluid waste material released by the kidneys

valve(VALV) — a flap between chambers of the heart that opens to let blood pass through, then closes to stop blood from flowing backward

veins(VANES) — tubes that carry blood from parts of the body back to the heart

ventricles(VEN • tri • kuls) — the lower right and left chambers of the heart

wastes(WAYSTS) — material that can no longer be used by the body

INDEX

About the author

Leslie Jean LeMaster received a Bachelor of Arts Degree in Psychology and has taken postgraduate courses in Clinical and Physiological Psychology. She has worked in the Child Guidance Clinic at Children's Hospital in Northern California, helping parents and children with behavioral problems to interrelate. Ms. LeMaster is in the process of completing a manuscript on an introduction to the human anatomy for middle grade-level children. She currently owns and operates her own business in Irvine, California, and is the mother of a nine-year-old daughter.